MELVIN LELAND

NETWORK MARKETERS

The Ultimate Guide to Network Marketing Lifelines, Discover Everything You Need to Know About Network Marketing Uplines and Downlines

Descrierea CIP a Bibliotecii Naționale a României
MELVIN LELAND
   NETWORK MARKETERS. The Ultimate Guide to
Network Marketing Lifelines, Discover Everything You Need to
Know About Network Marketing Uplines and Downlines /
Melvin Leland – Bucharest: Editura My Ebook, 2021
   ISBN

MELVIN LELAND

NETWORK MARKETERS

The Ultimate Guide to Network Marketing Lifelines, Discover Everything You Need to Know About Network Marketing Uplines and Downlines

My Ebook Publishing House
Bucharest, 2021

TABLE OF CONTENTS

INTRODUCTION
TO NETWORK MARKETING

Network marketing or Multi-level Network Marketing (MLM) is a method of marketing that makes use of independent sales reps as a way to reach a wider range of networks, where conventional methods such as traditional online or offline advertising wouldn't work. It is a very popular business opportunity for people looking to work part-time doing flexible jobs.

Hundreds of companies utilize this method, including some well-known brands such as Avon, Tupperware and Mary Kay Cosmetics: these companies and their respective associates hire a 'sales force', much like insurance companies have been doing for years, and they use these individuals to reach networks such as friends and family.

Ever come across an ad on TV using the term "Independent Insurance Agent", or something similar? These individuals are not really employees of the company; they operate independently by purchasing a product sample starter kit, which usually costs a few hundred dollars, and with that they get an opportunity to sell the product line to their own contacts, friends, family, etc.

These types of programs rely on an individual's ability to influence their network and sell products; and when properly executed, both parties benefit. Many network marketing programs require participants to recruit more sales reps, and as a participant adds to their own "downline", sales made by the new recruits generates income for those above them.

Compensation cannot be made exclusively on the basis of recruitment: instead, it should be based on the ability to sell company services and/or products. If a network marketing program generates revenue almost entirely from these recruitments then it may be illegal, and by definition would be a pyramid scheme.

A network marketing program is usually exempt from traditional business regulation and state and federal laws don't define it as franchises under franchise law, so you may need to do some research before putting in any money.

Why do businesses use network marketing?

It's pretty simple, they need to access your network, influence your family and friends, and traditional advertising methods tend to be limited. You would have an easier time trusting a new brand if a friend or family member suggested it, and that's what makes these programs effective.

The types of products and services included in a network marketing program can range from Nutrition, Finance, Communication, Internet Access, Electric Power, Weight Loss, etc. Word of mouth marketing is too powerful to ignore and because it's not as expensive as the alternative, which would be spending millions of dollars each year on complex marketing campaigns, companies are more than willing to pay you to spread the word.

The difference between a successful attempt at being a network marketer and a complete disaster doesn't necessarily depend on a person's ability to bug their friends, or lecturing them into submission to have them buying the product or service. That strategy might yield immediate results but it wouldn't work for long.

Your ability to learn who in your circles would benefit from what you're selling, and who would be interested in joining the program: that information will get you better results in the long run.

TYPES OF NETWORK MARKETING BUSINESSES

Most network marketing companies operate as some form of multi-level marketing plan, where the company provides a product or service and assigns agents to sell it. This setup gives the sales reps an opportunity to earn a commission by selling products, and recruiting new reps and growing their own little network.

Direct marketing works in a similar fashion, where a product line is launched to the market, and the company invests in a range of marketing materials including training and tools to help the new investors become successful. Commission largely depends on the number of items sold over a period of time and if there is an existing market to tap into, products can sell out in large volumes.

Individuals seeking out a more family-friendly type of network marketing could try out party plans, which are popular with parents who want an additional revenue stream. Party plan systems require an initial investment to create websites, buy product demons and relevant marketing materials, but their flexible scheduling makes them ideal for anyone splitting their time between the company and other responsibilities.

Technology allows sales representatives to expand existing networks and tap into new ones in order to establish a wider revenue stream. As their down-line expands, so does the commission and with a big-enough down- line your leg work reduces and you start earning from the new reps. But before you get to this point, you have to select the right type of system and have a plan of action.

The different types of networks

Here are the different structures available in network marketing:

1. Unilevel Structure

This system allows you to earn from your frontline and it doesn't limit the number of people you can sign. It's a pretty old system and it's certainly not the most lucrative but it does promote cross-line competition, which means a higher chance of expansion.

2. Stair Step Breakaway Plan

Perfect for the aggressive marketer, this plan is excellent if you have plenty of time to dedicate to sales. The higher you go up the steps, the more you break up from your own up-line, and in the end you'll only have people on your down-line, which means people will stop earning from you. If for instance you're supposed to breakaway at step 7, your up-line won't earn from you anymore, and you will get all commissions from anyone below you.

3. The Binary System

This system has been popularized by Questnet and it takes significant dedication to earn from. You only get two down-lines with this plan and new sign-ins are automatically under your down-line. In order to make money you have to earn from both down-lines; so when picking out this type of plan, try to get one where you can carry over extra points from the less active binary side.

4. Forced Matrix Plan

This system aims to promote teamwork and it allows newcomers to earn high commissions by combining forces with fellow members. Because it has a defined frontline, the system allows members to focus on signing more people in order to earn on higher levels.

HOW TO FIND THE RIGHT NETWORK MARKETING BUSINESS

If you'd gotten into network marketing a few years ago, there were very few companies doing it and back then people didn't spend weeks trying to find the right type of marketing business. But that is not the case today and in order to achieve any kind of success you have to be with the right company. There are literally thousands of companies available and new ones are popping up every other week, so the job of choosing the right one won't be easy.

One of the ways many people get into network marketing is because a friend or family member introduced them to a company but often this is not the best way because the company might not be suited for them. The result, often times, is frustration, failure or moderate success; all of which can be avoided.

Working with the right company doesn't automatically guarantee success, but it certainly increases your chances of attaining it. Ultimately what makes a person successful in network marketing is what they do, and that means building a network of people keen on purchasing a product or using a service. It's simple enough; you only need to provide information about the product or service, answer whatever questions your prospects might have, make the sale, do a little follow-up, sponsor them, train and support. Your passion for the job and desire for success will make all this simple and fun, and there's no way to get to that place if you don't believe in the company you work for. As a network marketer, you want to feel secure in the company, and for financial reasons you want to believe that it will be there for years to come, supporting you and your family.

So how do you get around to choosing the right company for you?

There are dozens of factors to consider but some people only need a few assurances before joining a company. We'll look at a number of issues just to make sure you are covered.

1. How long has the company been around for?

In order to make sure the effort you put in today will pay off for many years to come, select a company that's proven to be durable. This shouldn't be too difficult to work out: majority of network marketing companies, about 90%, fail within the first two years. Nobody wants to invest their time and energy into a company that can't guarantee continuity, so start by looking at this and you will shorten the list of companies significantly.

2. Are they well capitalized?

In simpler words, you're trying to find out if they have the cash needed to grow, bring in talented management, develop solid infrastructure, keep up with technology, and of course, pay your commissions. One way to make sure no company gets past your radar is to focus on public traded companies for the sole reason that they are required to disclose their finances to the authorities. Some of this information might be harder to access when dealing with private companies, so keep that in mind.

3. Is there a need for the product or service?

There are many horror stories about people who wasted their money purchasing products they don't really need. To avoid all the drama that comes with that, find out if whatever the company is selling fills a genuine void, if it actually helps people, and if it comes at a reasonable price. The product should provide value to the customer; otherwise the whole plan will fail.

4. Trend or fad?

Some products hit the market and generate huge waves of customer appeal but only for a short time, until they fade out. You might be able to make a good amount of money while the excitement goes on but the problem is you can't create any long-term residual income on a product that lasts a couple of months before fading off into oblivion.

Consider the long-term effect and find out if customers would be interested in using the product or service for a long time, that way your income won't run out.

5. Are you able to generate immediate income?

This would pay off if you're keen on expanding your network but the only way to ensure you get ready cash flow is to tap into an existing market. If you can locate a large untapped market for your product, that would be a good place to start.

6. Technology

Not everyone has fun doing sales work, but anybody can appreciate working in an environment that involves plugging into a system and using a bunch of tools to do the sorting and selling for you. Technology can be used to narrow down the targets and make your work a whole lot easier.

One advantage of having machines do the heavy-lifting is it allows you more time for yourself, and if you have another job to get to but don't want to lose money on either side, then it's perfect.

7. Are you working with a sponsor or recruiter?

The person who introduced you to this business opportunity could determine to a large extent, your success or failure. In addition to the company being strong and successful, you also require coaching, training and motivation, and your sponsor would be useful with that. Recruiters tend to abandon people as soon as they sign them.

8. How will you fit in with your business partners?

Although compatibility isn't the first thing many people consider when looking for a job, it should be important too. If you don't feel like you fit in with your co-workers then that takes the fun out of the job, and with that your passion to excel.

Start with the basics

This is a lot of information to go through and it can get more complicated if you don't really know how or where to begin. Let's try a step-by-step process and cover the areas you should start with:

– Research the company-this is where you find out how long they've operated, your potential for success, etc.

– Look for a product or service you like

– Carefully examine the company's payment plan

– Find out if you will get help with marketing. Some companies offer a wide range of tools including DVD presentations, associate websites and a range of marketing pieces

– Training - they should offer an associate training kit, and it helps if they have online tools, conventions and conferences to go along with it

Payment

Some areas will be more important in the long run and therefore require a deeper analysis. For instance a company's payment plan should be right up there. You will have four plans to choose from- Binary, Stair Step Breakaway, Matrix and Unilevel. You can spend hours studying these payment plans trying to figure out which one wouldn't disappoint, or you could just believe that they all work.

Provided a company has been in business more than a couple of years, all the payment plans would have to work, so what you should be looking for is a plan that allows you to sponsor more people. It makes a huge difference being able to sponsor an extra person so push for that higher number.

Timing

When seeking out a company, you want to avoid the startups but you also need to avoid companies that have been doing it for two decades. Large companies don't provide the best opportunities for someone who's starting out in network marketing. Think of it like a tidal wave, you want to ride the wave, not be too far behind or too far off in front before it gets going.

Products

As a network marketer you will have to choose from a variety of products, some good and others not so much. When you have the option of selecting from fields such as gas, electricity, telecommunications, personal care, household products, etc., how do you know what to go for?

What you have to check for is consumable products. You want products that customers buy month in month out, whether their paychecks go up or down. Think of hair shampoo vs. frying pans: one product has repeat customers and the other gets sold once.

So there it is; a whole bunch of criteria to consider when choosing a company to work with. Of course there's no such thing as a perfect company, but you can make progress if you find one with the least amount of problems.

HOW TO PRESENT
AND SELL YOUR PRODUCT

When starting out in network marketing you may be told to fiercely pursue everyone you know, and that everyone wants the products you are selling. Your up-line might insist that you go after your family and friends and have them buy the product whether or not they think they need it. The problem with this strategy is that it's entirely wrong and it's one of the many reasons some people fail to make it in this business.

When people get into network marketing with false expectations they soon realize they can't meet their goals and when things don't materialize, they blame it on the sponsors, the products, company and/or their bad contacts. Consider how mainstream business works; no one would ever attempt to force people into buying products they don't understand or have any use for. Yet that's what many people are trained to do.

Think of it this way; anyone can get into network marketing and make money, but different companies and products are not suitable for everyone. These products are broken down into 'niches' and this helps determine which area you fit into. Let's say for instance one company focuses on women's bikinis; how much trouble do you think the mechanic next door would have selling the products?

It would be a terrible combination because the auto expert can't familiarize with bikinis and therefore can't get comfortable selling them.

Most of us know someone involved in MLM or network marketing. It is a fantastic way to introduce products to the market without being at the mercy of the retail distribution system which favors large, established brands over little-known startups. As opposed to giving the shop owners and distributors the trade margins, the sales agent earns this for their contacts and of course the sales they make.

But MLM isn't at all a simple and straightforward business. Like any system that has the potential to generate huge sums of money, it tends to be slippery at times. Quite a number of people who've had experience in this industry can testify to losing a few friends for MLM companies when they insisted on making the products a part of the relationship.

That tends to complicate things and if every phone call happens to be a masked sales pitch, then you will definitely lose a few friends. The only way a friendship can work in such a situation is where your friend happens to be a distributor for the same company, and one of you is in the other's down- line. But if one person doesn't have anything to do with network marketing they won't be accommodative of a conditional friendship. This is why many people selling products in MLM end up with an elaborate network of friends - most of whom are fellow MLMers.

Persuasion

The reason why network marketing works so well is that most people have an easier time trusting a sales pitch from a relative or friend than they would with a stranger in a shop somewhere. The home setting also helps put people at ease, so that a stranger in a home setting has a better chance of selling a product than if they approached a target somewhere else.

Because of traditional forms of selling, most people are always on guard and will automatically put off any approach when in certain environments. MLM offers a form of sincerity and openness that makes it possible to pitch a sale when that guard is down and walk away successful.

Sell the product

Now when it comes down to it, you will need a set of instructions to help get you on track. Here's how you begin:

1. Identify your target market

Before you start distributing the products you have to start by establishing who you're selling the products to. The product you're selling will determine the market you have to deal with, so pick out the right product for you. If you find a company that sells products you can identify with, then that would be a good place to start.

2. Passion helps

You will come across challenges when growing your network but with proper motivation you can work through it. Some people are passionate about health products and can manage to sell to their networks at high prices regardless of the thousands of health products available at lower costs. Find something you're passionate about.

3. Make use of social hangouts

Find out where your target audience hangs out and join them. By making more friends, you will have a larger pool of prospects to tap into whenever you need to expand your reach. Popular social network platforms are a great place to recruit.

4. Always ask for referrals

If you find you're not making any progress with prospects, it could be that you haven't learnt how to use referrals. Talk to people you've sold the products and have them suggest people who would be interested to purchase from you. If you're selling a good, useful product it shouldn't be too difficult to locate someone happy to offer referrals.

5. Attend relevant events

Whatever approach you have to this business, you have to expand your social network and that means going out there and meeting new people. It shouldn't be a bore; most people have fun making new friends and learning about different backgrounds. Try to broaden whatever social structure you have and accommodate more people. Remember, you're not pushing people to buy your product; instead you are a fun and lively person with a new product most people would find useful.

6. Throw a party

If you're having trouble connecting with the guys at those events, how about you bring the party to you? Have all your friends and relatives bring their own friends, people you don't know, and let people know about your business. When you leave a party, make sure you have three more parties planned. That way you will grow your business faster.

7. Educate yourself

Learn about new and different ways to market your product. Some people are great at direct selling, but aren't too great with computers. Commit some time to learning how different technologies would benefit your new business, and be open to adjustments. If you fall apart every time you try to talk to customers, then perhaps a class on communication would be useful.

8. Remember ethics

This industry is littered with unsavory characters and these people will do or say anything to land a new sale. You might encounter some pressure while gearing for MLM success but try to run the business above bar where it counts.

9. Listen genuinely

Telling isn't really selling and if your conversations fly right past you, then you are not paying attention and you will miss out in the end. Show that you genuinely care what the customer thinks about your products and find a way to connect with them.

10. Share the business creatively

It's true you don't have to sound like a telemarketer every time you mention your business to friends or family. Be creative in how you introduce the business and products, and aim to be invaluable rather than intolerable.

Your job doesn't stop when you get enough customers and your own distributors: there's still more to do.

Send a monthly e-newsletter to your customers and inform them of special deals and any relevant information about the products. Make sure you keep a contact list and find a smart way to contact people when they go silent for a while. If your budget allows, pay for advertising so your new venture gets noticed.

TECHNIQUES TO FOLLOWING UP
WITH YOUR PROSPECTS

The follow up is in fact the most important part of the prospecting process so you need to give it some thought and time to make sure you get it right. We discuss a number of important points everyone should consider when preparing to follow up with prospects-a process that tells you whether you can form a long lasting business relationship with the prospect.

1. Sorting them out

We've already talked about how important it is not to grab everyone who shows interest in the team. Just make sure you know why you are taking in a new recruit because if you know their skills then you can put them to good use. In this business you sift and sort, not convince.

2. Edification

When first starting out, it's a good idea to have an experienced up-line or mentor to assist you with prospecting and follow-up. If you are meeting someone for the follow-up it wouldn't hurt to bring a long a more experienced member. This will help boost your conversion rate and make you an expert within no time.

Before you drag your mentor to your next meeting, contact the prospect and let them know you intend to bring someone to the meeting. It would help if you mentioned some of the accomplishments your mentor has in the industry, and encourage the prospect to ask questions. If the follow-up is done through a phone call, you can ask them to join in on the three-way call, it works just as efficiently.

That process of highlighting your team mates' achievements is what's called edification and it helps build respect as your prospect learns more about your supportive network.

3. Remember what you're selling

Try to recap on some of the basic marketing principles we mentioned earlier on; unless you're trying to convert existing network marketers, you have to know that your prospects are not really focused on the fancy products or the smooth compensation plan; what they want is a solution to their problems. This is what you need to target when doing the follow - throughs.

At the end of the day, that compensation plan is essentially a vehicle the person will use to solve some of their existing problems. When selling a business model some sales agents assume that prospects want in simply because they can make extra money. While the cash might be a good incentive, it is also important to make the solution client-specific. Find out what that extra money could do for the prospect, and you have a decent angle to work from.

4. ***"In the warehouse we make cosmetics, in the stores we sell hope" - Charles Revlon***

Because you want to be more effective and succeed better with the prospects, you will have to be more specific when tailoring that solution. For instance, the family may have planned a trip to Disneyland but never got to go, or perhaps the family has been eyeing that perfect dream house by the beach: whatever the dream is, you need to make it a possibility. This is why you need to know your prospects well. Look out for specific emotional phrases and use them to tailor a fitted response.

5. Leadership

We've mentioned self-assurance and how crucial it is when building the team. It's also important when you approach a follow up which is why you need to believe in the company, the product, and the dream it sells. Don't let the questions throw you off, just stick what the opportunity can do for the prospect, and if there's something you don't understand, it would be the best time to let your more experienced mentor interject.

Closing the deal

This is the best part of any business transaction and more so in network marketing, but keep in mind the relationship doesn't end here, and you will continue to interact with the person long after you get them on your team. The rapport stage is simple enough because people love to talk about themselves but at some point you will have to steer the conversation to the direction you want.

"The reason I'm calling you is to ask if you had a chance to review the information I gave you?"""

If they forgot about that, chances are they are not remotely interested in what you're selling. It's one of the processes people use to sort out the masses. If, however they made time to read the material, then you can move on to the next step. One of the concepts behind successful follow- ups is to make sure the prospect thinks about the positive aspects of the business opportunity, whether those positive aspects are accurate or of their own interpretation.

By asking the right questions, you can steer the conversation in the right direction and have the prospect focusing on what's important- that is, the remediation of their immediate problems. Some individuals tend to keep an open mind when faced with new experiences and challenging opportunities and this makes it easier to sell the idea. Not everyone is built that way and you will come across rigid people who approach business with a narrow focus. Try not to get rattled when your ideas get challenged.

What to expect from the follow up process

Ideally, you want to get back with that person or couple as soon as possible, preferably within a few days, while the idea is still fresh on their minds. You also don't want them to talk to the wrong people and get some negative feedback about the industry. It would be harder to get them past this if the feedback came from close friends or family.

The follow-up process can take anywhere from a few days to several weeks and in some cases, you can go for months or even years building friendship and the dream, until the time comes for them to join you.

General guide

– Book the next follow-up at the conclusion of the plan.

– Ideally, you should follow-up within 2 days.

– You may do the follow-up yourself or have your sponsor assist you.

– Start by building a friendship with the prospect. Do this by taking a sincere interesting their dreams, their goals, and their daily life. The stronger the friendship, the stronger the trust and respect you will have for each other.

– **Build them a dream.** Dreams inspire people and stimulate action. Find out what their dreams are and what their immediate goals are.

– **Train them.** Information is very powerful and intelligent decisions are not made in a vacuum. Learning about network marketing will give them understanding and when they combine that with the realization that their dreams are achievable, a spark will have ignited

10 WAYS TO BUILD
YOUR TEAM & FIND PROSPECTS

For a lot of first timers, their eventuality is as predictable as it is preventable. The prediction is that most of the recruits will drop out and find something or someone to blame for it. How many times do you hear people say "It took too much time", or "No one really helped me"? It happens way too often and this needn't be so.

There's a better way for you to build your empire as opposed to going one- step-forward, two-steps-back. Now, I am not saying that all you need to do is sponsor five or six individuals and teach them how to sponsor five or six more individuals- that's a lousy plan. What I'm saying is, in order to gradually and consistently grow your business you have to get to a place where sponsoring becomes and on-going process like eating or sleeping; essentially a part of life.

Growing the team

Prospects who go on to build big businesses have one thing in common- they are progressively educated on network marketing and as a result they become better leaders. A well-intended business idea and all the zeal in the world couldn't compare to a proper instruction plan to help forge the recruits into leaders.

Above-average success in network marketing requires among other things, belief in,

- the profession
- the business-building system, and
- the fact that you are capable of achieving success

You might be wondering why, if this is all true-and it is-, why then do people seem surprised when half their recruits quit for no good reason. We should be systematically instilling this information into the business builders so they don't all quit the first time they hit a rough patch. These ten points should help clear things out.

1. Aim to help people

A genuine desire to help people succeed is especially important in the initial stage when you're still trying to find a balance between sales and recruitment. It will mean more to your team if what they're selling makes life easier for someone. If people see you genuinely helping, then the responses will be more positive. The longevity and effectiveness of this system depend on how much value you provide and how helpful you are.

It's unlike conventional affiliate marketing when the commission comes in.

2. Duplication

After you develop an effective process of selling products and winning people, the next best thing is to find a way to duplicate that process. You will earn based on how successful your team is. So basically when you train the team and teach them to recruit reps, you earn off a percentage of their results, and this goes on and on.

3. Communication

Some people would argue that the best way to build your team is to communicate constantly. While we can all agree that communication is essential to growth, the more crucial element would be a working system. Put in place a system that works and have the team follow it. Some members will probably need more help before they find their way and for this you have a host of online tools to facilitate communication.

You can make regular Skype calls to give valuable advice on how to build strong teams, and you can use this as your sales pitch when recruiting.

Just talk about how your success is tethered to the team's capacity to work as one, and don't forget to mention that you can help them succeed.

4. Work with small groups at a time

If you have people coming up to you at social functions asking to join your team, then by all means, make time for them. Every new person you sign in is your responsibility. They will look to you for structure, instructions and they will expect you to make them successful. When this happens too often you might find yourself stretched too thin and your team will suffer because of it.

5. Help the recruits grow

Invest as much time as needed on your recruits and encourage them to use their knowledge to grow. When training them you will need to go beyond payment plans and the products. Self-development is what's needed in order to see a difference. Offer them tools and resources for training and get them to focus on developing as a unit.

6. Expanding further

At some point the paychecks and your inspiring words may not be enough to keep the team working at their best. When distractions come in and people start getting lazy, that's when you focus more on fresh recruits. Just as you did with the older guys, train the new guys and try to find that natural skillset which makes a recruit stand out and teach them how to use it.

7. Employ multiple strategies

When training your team, you want them to stick to a system that can be duplicated multiple times and generate results. One of the ways you can do this is to train them to work both long games and short games. These are essentially tactics people use to get immediate (short game) or longer lasting (long game) results.

For instance, you can start blogging right away but it will take time before you see good results. For the sake of creating a more effective system for your team, you need to combine both long and short term tactics and your team should be able to roll out a plan and see it through.

8. Sifting and sorting through the masses

When moving your prospect through your prospecting formula, don't be afraid to disqualify them if they fall short of your requirements. Although some people start off completely psyched, not all of them have what it takes to stick it out so worry about who you devote your time to. You should be looking for smart, motivated individuals who can work together and yield positive results.

9. Use online tools

Because everyone is constantly rushing, at some point you may have to use online tools to keep them busy and learning. Find good eBooks on network marketing and have them refer to these tools when they come across challenges. If they are motivated, they will uncover more tools online to help them grow, and your job will be a lot easier.

10. Social proof

As a professional marketer you will be required to interact personally with your team as well as new people. It's a way to establish rapport and build trust and it goes a long way in keeping the team functional. Plan early and keep your time. If a meeting is set to begin and end at a certain time, try to work within that specified timeline. It sends the wrong message when the team can't keep time.

Different home-based companies use different tools and strategies to extend their reach and sell their products or services. Find what works best for your company and develop a simple daily method that generates results, and then train your people to duplicate that process.

RECRUITING LIKE A PRO

Like any other industry, you will need to learn some skills in order to grow the business and achieve success. The more you learn about network marketing and all its elements the more likely you will build great residual income for you and your family. In order to make this work, you have to work past the three common elements: prospecting, presentation and duplication. But like many business owners, you may find yourself with a large number of recruits who are doing, well, nothing.

Unfortunately for many reps, the quick solution to this problem is to hire more people, and this rarely solves the problem; so you may find yourself operating on that principle of "get them in the front door faster than they leave out the back".

In order to get anywhere, marketers need to acquire posture or confidence. Far too many sales agents find themselves rolling out the red carpet for their prospects and doing all sorts of favors. The problem with this strategy is it sends the wrong message because who really wants to work with a wimp? Everyone wants to work with a confident, inspiring character; someone who's ready to go where no one has dared before.

This does not mean faking people out; its more about creating an image that gets you a positive response from your prospects. If you want to be followed as a leader, then you may have to act the part. Of course this doesn't mean you can go out and hire people indiscriminately, you still have to consider the type of person you recruit.

How many of your recruits quit right after signing up? It could be due to the fact that you haven't perfected your process but you can work on it. When going into the cold competitive market, connecting with people will be tougher than you can imagine but there are things you can do to break the ice.

I mentioned using posture when talking to people. Posture is crucial when you're trying to establish yourself as an authority on a subject but it shouldn't be used exclusively. When talking to people, try being attentive and smile more. This will change the tone of your voice and add to the effect of your words.

If you have to make cold calls then you have to control the way your voice sounds to the other party and find a quick way to build rapport. One of the ways you could do this is to find something you have in common with the prospect and use it as a basis to connect with them. Conduct a little basic research before calling people and find out something you two have in common, if you can't find a starting point then use your posture to create a comfortable environment by easing into the conversation.

It doesn't hurt to expose the business to as many people as you can, but that can be exhausting if you're just swinging for the numbers. When you come face-to-face with a prospect, you have to see things their way in order to present them something they find interesting. In order to get there and recruit like a pro, use these tips:

- What's in it for me? It doesn't matter how excited you are about a product or a business idea, if the other person doesn't see how they benefit from it, then you are just wasting time. Find out how your plan could benefit your prospect and you'll get their attention.

- Ask to use their first name. When answering questions, refer to them by their first name but remember not to overuse their name.

- Questions will work for you both. The prospect might bombard you with questions at the start but you don't have to discuss every aspect of the business at the first encounter. Certain questions when directed to a prospect tend to yield the right responses: for instance, "If you had financial freedom, how much more time would you have for your family?"

- Take a team member with you. You might hit a few obstacles if you come off as a lone ranger working in a difficult industry. If the prospects think what you're doing is too tough or scary, you might lose out. When you bring your sponsor with you it gives them some comfort because they have to do some recruiting in the future and they would feel better with a team member next to them.

- Don't get too desperate. At some point you will get desperate and a little frustrated when people don't sign off immediately but for the sake of your image, try not to show it.

- Don't argue with prospects. You can't always see things eye-to-eye with prospects. MLM has had its fair share of misfortunes especially when unscrupulous individuals develop clever methods to rip people off. Some of this negativity has made it more challenging to recruit people, and you will come across people with reservations about the concept of network marketing. When that happens, don't waste time trying to get them on your side, just move on.

What are some of the challenges people face when recruiting?

One of the main problems is the fact that every network marketer wants to avoid pain, indulge in please and find the path with the least resistance and sail all the way to Financial Freedom. The idea here is that you can find three people in your own little network of friends and family, recruit them and have those three people find three more people each and so on; gradually building the business empire you deserve. It's a cute idea but you know in order to successfully build an empire you will need a solid plan and some self-discipline.

It would help if you set up your mind to work hard before getting into this business because that's how it's done. Program your mind this way:

- Numbers don't lie and you will need to talk to many people.
- A huge number of your recruits will drop out faster than you can say training program.
- When you do finally get a few people working under you, they will more than likely to pull off 50% of what you do right and 100% of what you do wrong.
- If you haven't had your best recruit quit on you, then you haven't been in the business long enough.

These people working under you have to be inspired by you. Chances are they won't all put in 100% dedicated so don't give them a reason to drop out. If they see you stop recruiting directs, can you guess what will happen?

Why personal recruiting is still a big problem

It should be perfectly clear by now that personal recruiting is the most crucial skillset for this business. It determines to a large extent the success of the business but most people still struggle with it. Why is this? Because of the nature of personal recruiting, we can assume that some of the reasons people fail to recruit boil down to fear.

But it doesn't end there. When you speak to some of the more successful network marketers, they will tell you they struggled with the same problems but at some point decided the real reason they failed was laziness.

While we can empathize with a single parent who has to juggle between two jobs and a host of bills, but these reasons will not get you any closer to your goals and in order to see change, you will have to give more of yourself.

9 out of 10 reps are lazy and operate on a self-fulfilling prophesy that says "I can't do it".

Train yourself to recruit on command

You should start by working on your mind. Getting others to believe in you will be more challenging if you haven't quite learnt how to believe in yourself. You can work on your mind and mold it to be what you want by practice. Think of your mind as a glass of water, and your negative thoughts as dirt or grime in the water, now you want to clean your thoughts but can't really empty your brain, but you can pour in clean water consistently - positive reaffirming thoughts, emotions and images- until the water gets clean.

As you continue training yourself some of the more common fears and obstacles will clear out and you will get to a place where nothing limits your potential to recruit. Just do what you know you should be doing. A healthy attitude looks like this:

- I've done this before and it worked!
- It wasn't nearly as difficult as I thought!
- If I did it once I can do it again!

HOW TO HELP NEW RECRUITS
GET STARTED RIGHT

Want to know the most crucial time in a recruitment process? The first week pretty much determines how the rest of the course and indeed, partnership works out. But really it's the first 72 hours that are most crucial in a consultant business. The sad news is majority of the people who join a direct selling business actually "check" out mentally within the first three days, so all the training you do after that falls on deaf ears.

This is terrible news for anyone hoping to light up the world with their little marketing team, but of course it's not the end of the story. If you're a leader, or working on becoming one, then the first three days of signing a new member can have a significant effect on how that person performs in the business. It's a time where you want them to get off to a great start and stick it out when it gets complicated. Here are a few tips to help get them ready to sell more and exceed their own expectations:

56

The signup process

- Help them complete the signup process and advise them on any add-on items.

- Review the website with them and show them all the tools and resources available for training and any additional information featured.

- Agree on a launch date for the business and start working on a list of people to invite.

First 48 hours

- Illustrate reasonable business goals and help define their own. Each recruit has their own "why" and when you understand this, you'll know what to expect when they present the business opportunity.

- Make a customized calendar highlighting all the business meetings, personal and family activities, parties and other events over a period of at least two months. Remember to keep a few open dates in order to accommodate possible events.

– Get them excited about the new venture and have them invite their friends so you can present the opportunity to more people.

When they receive the kit

– If the new recruit lives nearby you can have them bring over the kit and review it together. If that is not possible then have him or her review the paperwork.

– Get the recruit prepared to do their first solo presentation - several materials will be needed here, including catalogues, business materials, email, phone numbers, etc.

– Review the presentation with each recruit so they know which order to present the opportunity.

After first presentation

– Meet them in person or over the phone and review how to submit the order to the company.
– Review the party and consider the attendees, sales, bookings, recruit leads, etc.
– Involve an expert in these meetings.

These steps will make it easier for the new consultants to duplicate the process with their own recruits, which will set you apart and ensure your team exceeds the company's fast start, setting you up for success. Keep it as simple as possible, and get them going right off.

Getting the team to start out strong can be difficult but not impossible. It has a lot to do with the individual recruit and their own will. What you want here are people who want to succeed and will do everything in their power to win. It is not enough for a person to want to try the business and see how it goes; one has to have a will so strong it overcomes every obstacle for its fulfillment.

Have the new recruits fill out all the paperwork and get the ball rolling. Remember, just because a prospect doesn't sign up now doesn't mean they won't consider it a month or two from now, so keep a list of contacts.

Printed by Libri Plureos GmbH in Hamburg, Germany